Master The Card

Say Goodbye to Credit
Card Debt...Forever!

Joe Paretta

BALBOA.
PRESS

Balboa Press books may be ordered through booksellers or by contacting:

Balboa Press
A Division of Hay House
1663 Liberty Drive
Bloomington, IN 47403
www.balboapress.com
1-(877) 407-4847

ISBN: 978-1-4525-0085-0 (sc)
ISBN: 978-1-4525-0086-7 (hc)
ISBN: 978-1-4525-0094-2 (e)

Library of Congress Control Number: 2010915192

Printed in the United States of America

Balboa Press rev. date: 11/18/2010

To my wife, Jessica, for inspiring me to write this book. Your love and assistance are invaluable. I love you very much!

Contents

WELCOME

Congratulations! You are out of credit card debt!!

"What?"

That's right.

Your balance is zero…on MasterCard, Visa, Discover, American Express, all the department and specialty store cards, gas cards………………………..ZERO!

"How can that be? I owe $2,000 on MasterCard, $5,000 on Visa, $750 on Discover, and those are just the ones I remember right off the top of my head."

I know. Been there. You see no way out because all you *can* see are due dates and minimum payments. It's frustrating; it's overwhelming; at its extreme, it's scary. Maybe you're getting phone calls from collection agencies. They like to threaten, don't they?

"What can I do? Where can I turn?"

You can pay off the debt, and you can turn within.

Once I accepted the fact that I had gotten myself into credit card debt, I could start getting myself *out* of it. I could not start paying off my debt until I said, "The Buck Stops Here!" (that is, in my wallet).

Once I stood up, my credit card debt "fell down"….steadily, and eventually, rapidly.

"Did you get a huge pay raise to do this?"

No, I was a part-time teacher and tutor during most of this time.

"Did you get a huge gift from relatives to pay off some (or all) of this debt?"

No, in fact, I did not talk about this with family at that time because I was embarrassed.

For some of them, this book will be **the first** they've heard of it.

"So what did you do?"

First, I decided to wean myself off credit cards. I had to stop using them for *every little thing I bought*. I turned that thought into action…or "inaction." Before long, I went from using credit cards for the most minor purchases to hardly using them at all.

Prior to making up my mind, I would use credit cards at least fifteen to twenty times per month. In my first year of "recovery," I used my cards **a grand total of twelve times…for the whole year!**

No, I did not go "cold turkey" that first year, but that's OK. You can't completely change a habit overnight. Twelve times is certainly a step in the right direction. And guess what? I *did* go "cold turkey" during my second year and have done so at other times since then, too. I do use credit cards occasionally, but I don't remember the last time that I incurred a finance charge. Presently, I have a balance of zero on the two credit cards I carry.

Also, my FICO score was 820 the last time I checked. That is on a scale of 300 to 850 (with 850 being the best score that one can attain). I don't write this to impress you. I write it to show that with determination and persistence, you can be free of the albatross that is credit card debt. In fact, when I was mired in debt, I had no idea what my FICO score was (nor would I have wanted to know in all likelihood – it probably would have been down near the low end of the scale.) For more information on FICO and credit reports, go to www.annualcreditreport.com.

I *did* know what a minimum payment was. It was all I could afford. I did know what an "interest rate" was. I was quite familiar with numbers like 16.9%, 18.9%, 22.9%, etc.

Now, suffice it to say that my FICO score is my friend and interest rates are "strangers."

I did it! And *you* will too!!

That's where this book comes in. Becoming debt free is a step-by-step process. It takes time, determination, and a belief that you no longer have to be "a slave to the lender," to borrow from the Book of Proverbs in the Bible.

I have written this book to illustrate how I got out of debt. In chapters One through Five, I explain the proven methods that will free anyone from credit card debt, whether you owe $2,000, $20,000, more, or less. Then, beginning with Chapter Six, you'll see how much brighter your future can be! See how much more you can do...for yourself and others. Ultimately, you will see that your credit card debt has taught you a lesson. Remember when your parents and teachers used to say, "Let that be a lesson to you"? Well, *this* lesson is not meant to "hit you over the head" or put you on the entrance ramp for a guilt trip. It's meant to teach you that credit card debt is unnecessary and to inspire you to make it a thing of the past. Use the note pages provided at the end of each chapter to mark your progress.

I want to help you get out of credit card debt, just as I helped my wife and others get out.

That is – if you *want* help. There's an old adage – "When the student is ready, the teacher appears."

If you are ready, "class" is in session.

CHAPTER ONE

MIND OVER MATTER

"What's the matter?"

How many times have you heard *that* question? The most common response to that question is "Nothing," which frequently translates to "Leave me alone!"

Now, however, *something* is "the matter" and most importantly, you are facing it, and not hiding from it. GREAT!!

Maybe this credit card debt has been gnawing at you for a long time. Maybe it has frustrated you, angered you, but you didn't know what to do about it. Fear not! You are NOT helpless!! Others, like me, have climbed out of the debt hole and are now standing solvent...happy and at peace. You will, too!! This book will show you how.

The first thing to know is that this "climb from debt to freedom" is a psychological one. In fact, it's as much psychological as it is material; for some, it might be EVEN MORE psychological than material. By this, I mean that if you believe that you can be debt free, you will be. If you see yourself as debt free, you will be. Ask yourself what a life of debt freedom looks like *just for you*. How would you feel? How would you think? How would you act...on a *daily* basis? How much different would this life be from the one that you live now? Many people cannot imagine this type of life because all they've known until now is payments, overdue notices, collection calls, and at the very least a paycheck-to-paycheck existence. Of course, this weighs on your mind; it's how you've been conditioned for so long. So with knowledge and a determined effort to rid this toxin known as credit card debt from your life, your mindset will ultimately change from one of poverty to one of prosperity.

As you forge your way, there will be some days when you will feel great, like you are making *huge* strides toward "Zero Balance Land." And you are, simply because your thoughts are now focused on the positive, proactive steps that are required to reach solvency. Your actions then are "reflections" of your thoughts and when you progress with your goal in mind, there's only one way to go.............FORWARD!

Then there will be other days when you will want to "throw in the towel" and give up. The "unexpected" events of life happen and usually at the "wrong" time (like there's ever a *right* time for the problems of life). The car breaks down, your child breaks his/her arm, the water heater springs a leak, and (add your own items here). These are the circumstances that will test your endurance to see how "serious" you really are about getting out and staying out of credit card debt. This can happen at any time: as soon as you decide to begin your journey to freedom, when you have made a significant dent in your indebtedness, when you are nearing total freedom from debt or at any other point along the way. In other words, be ready *every day* to face this challenge. I'm not saying to *expect* it every day. You don't want to taint your voyage with negative thoughts, just like you wouldn't want to fear getting lost every mile of the way along a cross-country trip. However, be prepared. What will you do when these things happen? How will you *respond*? It's not a question of *if* these challenges occur; the question is, "*How* will you act *when* they occur?" It is a choice – will you be proactive or reactive? Will you remain victorious and positive and consider alternatives to encounter this unforeseen occurrence, or will you be a victim whose negativity blocks you from envisioning creative solutions to these events, solutions that will help you to avoid debt and keep you on the road to affluence?

Again, it is a choice.

Trust me, expect both types of days along the way. There will even be days when *you will not think about your debt at all.* Imagine! It might be hard to believe now, especially if you are a frequent card user who habitually "swipes" it for everything from a twenty-five-cent pack of gum to a $2,500 vacation. But yes, there will be times when your credit cards will NOT weigh on you. You will not think about using them, and you will not think about your outstanding balances. When this happens, you'll know that you are starting to get a handle on your card use, your overall spending, and simultaneously your debt load. You are reforming your habits. You'll realize that those little pieces of plastic are not necessary appendages. They are simply little annoyances which now have a gradually diminishing effect on your life. AWESOME!! That's a step in the right direction.

Let's have some *fun* as we embark on this journey together.

"Debt? Fun?!?"

Yes, let's make it a game – dare I say a "Mind Game?" The "Mind Game," however, has positive results. You are the only player; you make *all* the rules. There are *no* losers and only one winner........................YOU!!

In this game, you must first change your mind about credit card debt. Until now, you may have thought that you had to use your credit card many times during the course of the week or the month in order to make ends meet…or to survive. It *doesn't need* to be that way.

So the first "rule" is to *think about* how you use credit cards. It's possible that that "swiping motion" you've been making at cash registers all over town has become a "reflex action." It has become such a habit that you don't hear the trumpets blare or the chorus chant "CHARGE IT!" as that piece of plastic runs through that "friendly" device, which ultimately pushes you deeper and deeper into "the abyss." It has become a "mindless" habit. Now that will change.

To gain control of your spending, I highly recommend that you track your spending *in writing*. You want to make yourself accountable for every penny you spend. This may sound tedious at first, but like any habit, it will become second-nature once you get used to it. And whereas your habitual credit card use caused harsh consequences in your life, listing your cash purchases will be empowering because you will see *immediately* where your cash is going. It "hurts" a little when you spend cash; your wallet or pocketbook feels a little lighter. When we use cash, we actually have to part with something, and many of us don't like parting with our money. But this is really the only way to break our "reliance" on credit cards. So, writing down your purchases and their costs gets you thinking about what you buy and *why* you buy. This was the first proactive step I took once I decided that I was sick and tired of credit card debt.

So, here's my suggestion:

For two weeks (14 days), list *everything* that you buy and the *exact* cost of the item. I mean everything – to the penny. Don't round up or down. Be exact. Remember, we're replacing unproductive habits with productive ones, and you want an exact picture of what your spending looks like. So, be precise and accurate.

When should you start this practice? My answer is: "The sooner, the better!"

Some people are ready to start right away; others need a couple of days to get mentally prepared for this shift in consciousness and to prime themselves for jotting down all of their purchases. Decide for yourself when you want to start, but please do this. Once I got used to writing down what I bought and its cost, I started to like the process. I always had a pen on me anyway, so now I just had to get used to carrying around a little spiral notepad. Don't rely on your memory – you have a lot going on in your life between work, home, and other activities. As soon as you have paid for your items, write them all down. Don't worry about what other people might be thinking – they're probably in debt, too! The only difference is – YOU are getting out. Them? Probably not (at least not until they start making positive strides – like YOU!).

By focusing on cash payments and being diligent in listing my purchases, I saw that I could get through the day without using my credit card. I also started to cut out some unnecessary expenditures, like an extra cup of coffee or a bag of pretzels. I felt better about myself in the process.

Here is a look at one of my (partial) spending lists:

Monday, June 5

Breakfast (Egg on a roll and coffee) = $2.85

Gas = $5.00

Dinner (Turkey Hero) = $2.15

Tuesday, June 6

Breakfast (Pancakes and coffee) = $4.50

Lunch (2 slices of pizza and soda) = $3.24

Laundry = $8.00

Wednesday, June 7

Coffee = .85

Miscellaneous (Lottery) = $1.00

Lunch (Turkey & Swiss on rye, chips, coffee) = $5.62

Entertainment (Movies) = $8.00

Thursday, June 8

Breakfast (Bagel & Coffee) = $1.50

Newspaper = .50

Gas = $7.00

Groceries = $15.45

And the list continued in similar fashion. After several days of listing my expenses, I realized a few things: 1) it was easy to take a few seconds to write down these purchases, 2) I liked how it felt to "be aware" of my purchases, and 3) I spent a significant amount of money eating out. That has been reduced over the years, not eliminated (I do like to eat out occasionally), but now I keep a closer eye on this component of my spending.

Yes, you do need to go shopping *for the essentials* and it's OK to buy the **occasional** (please highlight, underline or put stars around that word) treat while you march towards your zero balances. I encourage you to treat yourself once in a while (not to a new jet-ski but to something small) so as to avoid falling prey to a poverty mentality. Now, you will think about *how* you will pay for things.

Suggestion...........................Pay Cash!

<u>Keep this in mind</u> – Nobody can get out of credit card debt by using their credit cards.

In essence, you will be trading one habit for another. You will get into a "cash habit" while breaking the "plastic habit."

<u>NOTE</u> – Not all habits are bad. By getting on a steady cash "diet," you will likely reduce your spending. You will think more carefully about your purchases than if you buy "on credit" and in relatively short order, your credit card debt will be reduced too, just as one's waistline reduces when he or she stays away from the junk food and makes a conscious effort to exercise – little things like taking the stairs at work instead of the elevator. You have to think about how you eat. You have to think about how you spend.

Once you start thinking actively about what you buy and how you pay for it, you will start gaining control of your spending habits. This realization will be empowering and you'll believe that you really can and will get out of debt.

You Win The Game!! It truly is a case of "Mind Over Matter."

Notes:

Notes:

CHAPTER TWO

BLACK AND WHITE

OK, so you're "in the red." What does that mean? You're in debt.

No, no, I'm not condemning you. Remember, I used to be in debt, too. I was once where you are now. And as I wrote in the introduction of this book, I will help you get out of debt.

However, in order to reach "Zero Balance Land," we must face facts. No one ever got out of debt using "the Ostrich Method" – that is, sticking his or her head in the sand and hoping the problem simply goes away. That might be "fantasy land," but *this is real life.*

But you already know that – so let's move on.

You must know *exactly* how much credit card debt you have presently…to the penny.

Studies show that most people with significant balances on their cards have little or no idea how much they owe. They estimate, they guess, they deny, but *they don't know.*

Frequently, debtors fall into one of three particular categories. One group approximates the amount owed (these people are often too low or even too high in their estimations.) Upon learning the actual amount owed, they realize that they'd "better do better" than take a "wild guess" about their balances.

Members of a second group, when asked how much they owe, look like the proverbial deer in the headlights as utter panic sets in upon hearing this question. Some even act as if a value judgment is being passed on them, or like the police have been called to "take them away" like criminals. <u>NOTE</u> – there is *no* debtor's prison. These people are scared, maybe guilty, because they don't know how much they owe. They use their cards "blindly" and have a vague idea that maybe they are approaching their credit limits on certain cards. Prior to the collapse of the financial industry in 2008, in these cases, a short phone call usually raised their available credit. Banks were only too happy to give these people more credit when they were making only the minimum payment and occasionally incurring the $29 or $35 late fee. The longer banks can keep you in debt, the happier they are. Banks are enablers in this case – credit is the "drug." If they see that you're "hooked," meaning you're a frequent "user" who seems unable to go without a "fix," they tempt you further, sometimes subtly, sometimes overtly.

So the question, "How much do you owe?" should serve as a wake-up call to people in this category.

A third group (the great minority) is composed of people who are able to say with certainty the amount that they owe. These people know, almost always to the penny, what their balances are and to whom this money is owed. This is not a "lucky guess." They keep close records, file their statements carefully, and pay their balances on time month after month. Regularly, they talk with their spouses, partners, children, or other trusted people about their finances. This creates an accountability factor which helps discipline these people to pay their bills.

In short, these people are "in the know." They take the time to maintain a handle on their finances and spending habits. It's no coincidence that they carry little or no debt most of the time, barring the unforeseen emergency. It's not because they are better than everyone else, or they make a six-figure salary. They've simply prioritized their finances and paid attention, instead of interest.

Our goal is to be a part of that third group. With the appropriate mindset and determined actions, you can be a part of that group.... if you truly *want* to be.

Now remember that in Chapter One, we established that getting out of debt is a game that you *will* win, so let's take our first proactive step in making this victory a reality. Likely, you've heard the statement "Knowledge is power." That is partly true. Yes, you need knowledge (or know-how) to get out of credit card debt, or to do nearly anything in life.

But without action, knowledge sits in your head, seeking an outlet. Knowledge is like water in a faucet. If you want a glass of water, simply knowing that water is in the faucet will not quench your thirst. You need to grab a glass, put it under the spigot, and turn the knob in order for the water to come out (and, oh yes, don't forget to drink).

Action steps are mandatory in order to arrive at your desired destination, whether it is to hydrate yourself or to eliminate your debt. So let's alter the statement to read *"Applied* knowledge is power." This foreshadows Chapter Five, but it's important to set out here that there will be some work involved when it comes to reaching solvency. But a little hard work is a good thing!

For now, though, our first step is to know what you owe *on each and every card.* So go to your wallet, purse, pocketbook, file cabinets, wherever you keep your cards. Gather and count how many cards you have and write their names on a piece of paper, in no particular order. This is just an inventory to make sure that every card has been accounted for.

Once you have done that, then take out your latest statements for each of these cards. You may find these where you keep your cards or they may be elsewhere. Just take your time and look for them. Frequently when we get overwhelmed by debt or try to deny its existence, we scatter our statements or put them where we cannot readily get to them. This is the "out of sight, out of mind" mentality in which we hope that our debts simply go away. That won't happen. However, the good news is that once we make up our minds to cut into our debts, our efforts/actions become concentrated and we replace the aforementioned "Ostrich Method" with "Eagle's Wings." You are ready to soar! Positive results follow. We install a system that allows us to easily oversee our statements. This means keeping them all in *one easy-to-reach location.*

Organization is key to gaining control of your debt.

Let's say you have four credit cards: one Visa, one MasterCard, one American Express, and one Discover Card. File their statements individually; do not mix them together.

Don't merge Discover with AmEx, for example. Instead, paperclip your Discover statements together, keeping the most recent statement on top. Do the same for each of the other cards' statements, too. And do this whether you have two cards, five cards, ten, twenty... anything in between or beyond.

It is crucial to stay organized! *Getting* organized is an important first step, but *staying* organized will empower and lead you to freedom!

At this point, you've gathered all of your statements...or so you thought. Maybe the number of cards does not correspond to the number of statements. Let's say you have more cards than statements. Don't panic – you can either call the Customer Service phone number that appears on the back of that particular credit card and request current statements or, thanks to the Internet, you can go to the bank/card Web site and see your statement on your computer screen.

OK – here we go! You've got the statements. Now, grab a pen, another piece of paper (separate from the previous piece on which you listed your credit cards), and a calculator.

Add up all of your current balances.

At this point, the interest rates do not matter. We're not concerned with finance charges at this time. We just want a grand total of what you owe.

Please read this next line *slowly* and, if necessary, *multiple times......*

******Do NOT let this step frighten you!******

This is one of the most important steps that you will take in our journey together. It's your starting point. You cannot get to point B without knowing where point A is situated.

You must know the *exact* amount you owe at the *present* time.

Without this knowledge, you will only be playing a guessing game, one which is difficult, and likely impossible, to win. And yes, you are creating the rules, but you want to put yourself on the right track so that you position yourself to succeed while simultaneously decreasing frustration and anger. Think, Act....And Win The "Mind Game" (Chapter One).

So, please take the time necessary to write down each of your balances, and add them up.

Here's an illustration:

MasterCard	=	$2,489.12
Visa	=	$1,312.03
Discover	=	$ 616.72
Am Ex	=	$ 557.24

$ 4,975.11

See – simple enough to do...and empowering. Now you *know* what you owe to the penny. Applied knowledge is power.

What did you come up with? $1,000? $2,000? $5,000? $10,000? $20,000?

More? Less? Somewhere in between?

It's OK. Honestly, the amount is important only because now we know where to begin. Instead of approximating our situation, we can say *with certainty*, "I owe $5,000," or "I owe $30,000," or "I owe fill in the blank."

Now you know. Maybe you feel a bit shocked, dismayed, horrified, or again, fill in the blank. That's normal; that's natural. In short order, those negative feelings will dissipate as you "role up your sleeves" and start digging your way out of debt. Remember, I'll be here to help you. "Two shovels are better than one!!"

Now that you have this grand total written down, *in black and white*, your situation has become clear and you're ready to proceed.

Notes:

Notes:

CHAPTER THREE

STOP!

"What? You just said, 'You're ready to proceed.' What gives?"

Nothing.

(By the way, to answer your question, we'll get to "Giving" in Chapter Six).

I figured this chapter's title would get your attention.

Now that we know what we owe and that we will win this game, one essential point needs to be reinforced...

As much as possible, STOP using your credit cards. If you recall, I wrote earlier that I did not go "cold turkey" immediately. There were times when I felt I *had to use* my credit cards, but the difference between "had to" and "*wanted* to" was like "night and day." Because I initially reduced my use of credit cards, I reconditioned my mind to realize that credit cards are not essential to my life. Certainly, they do not bring me happiness or the "status" that

I thought they did when I was so deep in debt. Ironic, isn't it? With my MasterCard, I felt like "a man about town." But there's a reason why it's called "MasterCard." If you are not careful, it will *master you*. That makes you its slave.

Think of how silly it sounds to be a slave to a piece of plastic with a magnetic strip and a series of numbers. But that's what happens.

And it's true for whichever cards you have (Visa, American Express, etc.) What do you discover with your Discover Card? That you are in debt, and hopefully you discover this "sooner rather than later" while your balance is still relatively low.

When I speak about debt during my seminars, I refer to credit cards as "plastic hand grenades." The only purpose of a grenade is destruction. You pull the pin, throw the grenade, and watch it decimate whatever (and whomever) it lands near.

Now think of your credit cards. All you do with them is go into debt… and maybe collect frequent flyer miles that most people never cash in. When you use these cards regularly, excessively, unconsciously, they too become destructive…to your income, happiness, and peace of mind, among other things.

Notice another similarity between the hand grenade and the credit card. The grenade has a pin that must be pulled before the damage is done. The credit card also has a PIN (Personal Identification Number). This number enables you to get a cash advance with your card, frequently at rates higher than those charged for the traditional swipe of the card. If you don't "pull the PIN" on your card, you can't get the cash…and that's a *good* thing. In effect, *it's not your money anyway*. In the long run, you'll need to repay *their* money with *your* money. Add the interest (more of *your* money) and that advance, which seemed so good and fulfilling at the time, further damages your savings. In addition, the interest rate for a cash advance well exceeds one's rate for purchases.

I remind my clients and audience members about the credit card/hand grenade analogy…and I suggest that they add sound effects to bring the point home. You can do this, too, in the comfort of your home or wherever you happen to be. Visualize a hand grenade. It fits in the palm of your hand (thus the name); it's round, kind of bumpy, and has that pin I referred to earlier, the only thing holding the explosive elements of that grenade together. See it; feel it. Now see yourself pulling that pin, throwing the grenade, and watching it hit its target. You see a cloud of smoke *and* you hear the explosion. Lastly, you see the destruction left in the grenade's wake.

At this point, I ask my clients or people in attendance to do an exercise with me. This, too, you can do wherever and whenever the need arises. I ask them to take a credit card out of their wallets, purses, etc. If they don't have a credit card with them (good for them; if they don't have it on them, they can't use it, and therefore, they cannot go further into debt), I suggest that they imagine themselves holding one. Then together, we pretend that we are on a checkout line, ready to complete a purchase.

On the count of three, we take our cards and we swipe them through the air (through an "invisible" scanner)…except this time as we swipe, I say the following,

"MasterCard" (and the sound effect)……BOOM!!!!!!!!

We do it a second time; this time I say,

"Visa" (and add)............CRASH!!!!!!!

The third time, I say "AmEx" and TOGETHER we all say AS LOUD AS WE CAN......

KA-BOOM!!!!!!

Actually, it's FUN! Many people laugh, but more importantly, they realize that credit cards run amok leave disaster in their wake, just as grenades do. Whether it is to land, buildings, people, or finances, devastation is devastation…and it is unnecessary.

So before you make your next purchase, before you reach for that card….

"STOP" and seriously consider *how* – and how much – you will pay for it.

Notes:

Notes:

CHAPTER FOUR

LET THE SAVINGS BEGIN!

OK – *now* we are ready to proceed.

Sorry about the "curveball" I threw you in Chapter Three, but it got your attention, right? Good! That's the point of all of this. To get out of credit card debt and eventually live a life of abundance requires awareness, a desire to STOP the unproductive habits, and replace them with prosperous thoughts and actions. This change begins in the mind as you admit that what you have been doing up to now has not been working. It has caused only hardship and frustration. But fortunately – I love that word because it has "fortune" at its root – once we realize that there is a better way, we can decide to change course and follow a path to prosperity.

It is likely now that you know (in your mind) that freedom from debt is possible. However, in your *heart and soul*, maybe you still doubt. Deep-seated habits can be hard to break. There may be some negative thoughts, such as, "I'll never get out of debt," or even, "I'll die before I become debt free." This reminds me of the "Angel"/ "Devil" scene that we used to see in cartoons when we were kids. The "angel" would hover over a character's shoulder, encouraging the character to do the right thing while the "devil" would hover over the other shoulder and tempt the character to do something that would bring "instant gratification" while, of course, omitting mention of "the price to be paid" in the near future.

If we are encouraged by our newfound head knowledge – that the reduced use of, or abstinence from, credit cards will soon lead to freedom from debt – then there is a *great* chance that our actions will follow those thoughts. On the other hand, if we "look in the rearview mirror" and focus only on our debt filled past and our mounting bills, then we will probably repeat the actions that got us into debt in the first place.

It's a thought…it's a choice…it's a decision…it's up to you. But remember, you now know a better way. It's NOT impossible. Remember that *many* people have climbed out of credit card debt and gone on to live enriched lives. I am one of those people. Some have even gone on to great riches and millionaire status.

And (believe it or not), some people have had even more debt than you have now and they still managed to become debt free. Some have paid off their debts while making less money than you make now. Still others have done it while having just a relatively small amount of savings. All this to say, "It's doable" (if you believe it).

I repeat – It's NOT impossible. In fact, take that word "impossible" and change it to read:

I'M POSSIBLE

See what we did. We simply made a couple of little changes. We put a space between the "M" and the "P," and we put an apostrophe between the "I" and the "M." Most importantly, we changed a negative to a positive! That's the ultimate goal of this process and of this book. Just a couple of changes in the way we think and the way we act make *all the difference*.

So with that in mind, let's act!

Back in Chapter Two, you gathered all of your statements and listed the cards and their balances. You also did some "housekeeping"; specifically you organized your statements and placed them in one easy-to-reach location. Please go there now and take out your latest statements.

Next, grab a pen or pencil and a pad of paper. Write down the interest rate for each of these cards *on separate sheets of paper*. For example, if you have seven cards, you'll need seven sheets of paper. There's a reason for this, which I'll get to momentarily, but for now, write the name of the card (i.e., "Chase Visa," "Bank of America MasterCard," etc.) and its interest rate at the top.

OK – if you recall earlier in the book, I mentioned that there is a telephone number on the back of your credit card which allows you to get in touch with the "Customer Support/Service" department. That number should also appear on your statements. Starting with the card that has the *highest interest rate*, call the Customer Service department and *negotiate* a lower rate. Yes, you can do this: it is legal and you have the ability ("guts") to do it. The card companies count on the general public to be lazy or believe it is helpless against "the giant banks and card companies." NONSENSE!

You're about to do it – you're about to negotiate.

Webster's Dictionary defines the word "negotiate" as "to confer with another so as to arrive at the settlement of some matter." It also states "to get through, around or over successfully."

You can see, based on the latter definition, that there are various ways to overcome obstacles. But you MUST be proactive. So, pick up the phone and dial that toll-free number. You *will* "get through" to a representative and your goal is to "confer"/talk with as many people as it takes until you "arrive at the settlement... successfully." That is, you'll *negotiate* until you are offered a lower interest rate on that particular credit card. If you have a history of making payments on time, you improve your chances of securing a lower rate.

Some people stumble or hesitate, at least initially, at this stage. They say things like, "Oh, they're in it for the money. They'll never go for this." Or there's, "I couldn't do that. I'm not a 'phone person'" (whatever that is). Even, "My friend tried this, and they laughed at him!" Well, I mean no offense to your friend, but you're *not him or her*, and you are *serious* about getting out of debt, sooner rather than later.

So grab the phone and make that first call.

Remember those separate sheets of paper – one for each card? Beneath where you wrote the card's name and interest rate, take notes of your conversation with the representative(s). You may be talking to a few people concerning the interest rate. Taking careful and consistent notes helps you stay organized. *Do not rely on your memory and say to yourself, "I'll write stuff down after I hang up."* You are a busy person with a lot on your mind. Note-taking is a foolproof method for keeping the details of the conversation straight, thus avoiding a "He Said, She Said" scenario between you and the rep. Also, keeping and reviewing notes will improve your skills when making such calls in the future, strengthening your ability to handle these situations if they arise with another representative or card company. If you have to jot down notes and comments quickly, that's fine. Just be sure that you understand your "scribbling." Accuracy is very important!

Immediately after the phone call, *rewrite* your notes (that's right – yet another piece of paper) so that they are clear to you. This also helps to refresh your memory regarding the main points of your discussion, and it allows you to see whether you may have neglected to ask or talk about something important.

Again, do this for every card that you carry.

Your phone call *might* begin with you speaking to a customer service representative who has absolutely no authority (or desire) to help you. Likely, this person is making about minimum wage (and carrying debt, too). The rep may say something like, "I'm sorry. There's nothing I can do for you." At this point, be polite but assertive. You must be a "self-advocate." Ask to speak to a supervisor – 9½ times out of 10, you will be transferred. On the "off-chance" that this does not happen, again because the rep really does not care about you (the phrase "Customer *Service*" is frequently a misnomer here), simply hang up and call again. This time, tell the new rep to transfer you to a supervisor immediately.

As each conversation progresses, you are recording the dates and times of the calls, the names of *all* of the people involved, specifically what you have requested, and how the reps have responded (word-for-word and attitude). Each rep should provide his or her name at the beginning of your conversation, but if this does not happen, ask for the name right away. Say, "Good Morning/Afternoon/ Evening…" (pick *one* so they don't think you're nuts!), "may I have your name, please?" You are putting forth a professional tone as you politely establish a rapport. Hopefully, the rep(s) will follow your lead. If not, maintain your positive attitude, but be firm until you get what you want. Work your way up the chain of command as far as you have to go to get what you want. Don't take "no" for an answer.

If you find that you're "getting nowhere" after having spoken to three or four representatives/supervisors at the same company, tell the latest person, "Look! I really would like to stay with you. But I have a chance to lower my rate to <u>(fill in the blank)</u> percentage by transferring my balance to <u>(fill in again)</u> bank. So unless you can match that offer or do better, I'm gone." Remember, this is business…and they don't want to lose yours! Chances are, they will work with you once you have used your "Ace in The Hole" (a.k.a. – your "new" offer).

I suggest that you don't tip your hand about another offer too early. Wait until you get to a supervisor or a manager and if that person isn't satisfying you, tell him/her about the balance transfer from X Bank…….guess what? Even if there is *no new offer*.

Let's not kid ourselves. For many years, the banks and credit card companies have been deceitful and "played dirty" with our money. They've unjustifiably raised interest rates "through the roof," they've deliberately withheld the posting of payments that arrived on time so that late fees could be charged (thank goodness for the Internet and the ability to pay online), and they've even cut available credit to those of us who use the cards "infrequently" or have a long history of prompt payments in full. They call us "deadbeats." Ironic, huh?

So "fight fire with fire." Take on Goliath! Be respectful, but firm. By doing this, I have won in the past and I believe *you will win, too!!* (**SEE CHAPTER 10 – "A FINAL WORD," FOR FURTHER INFORMATION REGARDING RECENT CREDIT CARD LEGISLATION THAT EMPOWERS THE CONSUMER.**)

One last item for this chapter – you may have to be on the phone several times in order to lower your interest rates. For example, if you have ten credit cards, all of which carry high interest rates, you will need to make at least ten phone calls to make headway. Factor in transfers to managers and higher-ups, and the time spent can be significant. IT'S WORTH IT! Think of all the interest you WON'T be paying in the long run!

The thought of making so many calls and speaking to multiple people can be daunting. Nobody said that you need to make all the calls in one day. So set a schedule for yourself. Again, using ten calls as our example, determine to make two calls a day for five days (or evenings). If you start on Monday, by the end of the business week, you will have accomplished your goal. Bravo!

Or maybe you feel that you cannot devote that much time in one week. OK – how about this? Make five calls this week, and five calls next week. You've still accomplished your goal; it simply took two weeks instead of one.

The key here is to *do it!* Get started – that is often the hardest part of the process. You want to build confidence and momentum when dealing with these people. Procrastination and fear are your "worst enemies" on this quest.

So Start. Start Now. You're likely to feel empowered as you realize that you took on the "Credit Card Monster"…AND WON!!

LET THE SAVINGS BEGIN!

Notes:

Notes:

CHAPTER FIVE

CHIP, CHIP, CHIP AWAY

How are you feeling? What are you thinking right now?

This is a good time to take your "emotional temperature." You have done a lot of work to begin moving yourself out of debt, so take a breath and congratulate yourself for the positive strides that you have taken.

"But I still have all this debt!"

That's OK. Look at how much has changed! You have accepted the fact that you have debt, you've committed to minimizing use of your cards, you've clearly listed each debt and its corresponding interest rate, and you've contacted the issuers and negotiated lower rates.

AWESOME!!

Take credit (yes, pun intended). It took a lot of courage and dedication to start turning around your situation, and it will take continued courage and dedication to make further inroads. But see how much you have changed since the beginning of this book. You've made up your mind to make your life better – financially, emotionally, and psychologically – and you've followed through. Keep going!

Back in Chapter Two, your "assignment" was to list, in no particular order, how much you owed on each of your credit cards. Now, let's go back to that list and work further on it. Specifically, let's alter the list so that now your balances read *from lowest to highest*.

For illustrative purposes, let's say that you have four credit cards, and your list currently looks like this:

Visa	=	$4,500
MasterCard	=	$6,000
Discover Card	=	$750
American Express	=	$2,000

At this point, rewrite the list so that it now reads:

Discover Card	=	$750
American Express	=	$2,000
Visa	=	$4,500
MasterCard	=	$6,000

The list is now written with your smallest balance appearing at the top, and your largest balance at the bottom.

This has a *significant psychological effect*. Frequently, we think about our debt as one lump sum and it overwhelms us. This compounds our doubts about getting out of debt and frustrates our liberation process.

By rewriting your list from lowest to highest, you train your eye *and your mind* to focus on the top (or lowest) figure first. Using our example, our eye falls on the number $750, the current balance on the Discover Card, which we can all agree is significantly lower than the grand total of your debt, whatever that happens to be. It doesn't really matter right now.

"$750. That's doable," you say to yourself, since you have stopped using the Discover Card and you have negotiated a lower interest rate.

You just smiled…faintly. But still, it's a smile. You realize that you haven't smiled very much recently, when you have thought about money and debt. This is a breakthrough! You have cleared a mental barrier as you realize that paying off $750 is a reasonable task. The best part is that it can be done in a relatively short period of time, even on *your* salary and savings.

When you have been weighed down by debt, the first thing you need (aside from money) is *hope*. You are gaining hope, and it will grow as you work through your debts. Hope truly does "spring eternal," and you are beginning to feel like "a new person."

Now get your list, a pen, and paper.

We need to determine how much money will be devoted to debt repayment each month. **Know that most banks consider a minimum payment to be about five percent of your card balance**.

BUT REMEMBER – we are going to pay *more* than the minimum on this card so we can pay it off as quickly as possible.

<u>My advice</u> – take the $35 minimum payment, 5% of the balance, and *double* it to $70.

To start, there is a $750 balance on the card. When you pay $70 per month for twelve months, factoring in the interest rate, you will have the Discover Card *paid off in fourteen months!* YES!!

Now you may be thinking, "Fourteen months!?! That's a long time!"

Well, look at it this way. If you continued to use the card, your balance would likely remain around $750, or, more likely, it would grow even higher.

Also, it took a long time to fall deep into debt; it takes a while to get out, too.

Instead of thinking about the time it takes to pay off the debt, think of how good it feels to see your balance drop.

Remember, too, that you have been paying the minimum on your other cards while throwing "extra" money at the Discover Card. Once Discover is "bye-bye," you can roll the money that you had devoted to that card over to the card with the next lowest balance. In our illustration, that is the American Express card.

Over the past fourteen months, you've paid $100/month to AmEx, which is 5% of the balance. The "bad" news is that your $2,000 balance has not gone down very much, only about $100. It's not much, but it's something. At least, the balance went down, not up. The credit card companies have "the deck stacked against us" when it comes to debt repayment. It takes approximately 20 years to pay off a $2,000 balance when only minimum payments are made.

The GOOD NEWS is that it will take *much less time* to pay off the AmEx balance now that the Discover Card is paid off. Now, we are going to take the $70 that was going towards Discover and add it to the $100 monthly AmEx payment. So, our new AmEx payment becomes $170/month. In the next twelve months, your AmEx balance will fall from $1902 to $573.66. (Again, this assumes that you are not using the card and you are paying the minimum to Visa and MasterCard).

See what happened? In the first fourteen months, you paid off just $100. However, in the next twelve months, the balance fell by $1326! Continue to pay $170 per month for another four months, and the AmEx balance will be *zero*!

OK – two down, two to go.

It took 30 months (2½ years) to pay off the first two cards in our example. Again, if you feel that this is "such a long time," ask yourself, "How much would I owe after 30 months if I continued using the cards and had no repayment plan in place?" Also, remember that it would take 20 years to pay off a $2,000 balance when just the minimum payment is made.

20 years = 240 months!

I'll take the 30-month plan, thank you.

Next comes the Visa, which originally had a $4,500 balance. If it takes 20 years to pay off $2,000, we would be "old and gray" before we pay off *this* balance. But not with our plan!

While we were focusing on paying off the Discover and American Express cards, we paid $225 a month towards the Visa (again, that's assuming a minimum monthly payment of 5%). Now, starting with our 30th month of debt recovery, that $225 monthly payment balloons to $395. How? We take the $225 from Visa and add the $170 that we had been putting towards AmEx. In the next thirteen months, the balance on Visa falls from $3763 to zero!

All tolled, the $4500 Visa balance is paid off in 43 months, or just over 3½ years, with the lion's share paid in the final 13 months, thanks to our repayment plan.

3½ years versus 40+ years...........ROCK ON!!

Lastly, it's time to tackle our final credit card – the MasterCard. Our minimum payment is $300 per month on the $6,000 balance. While paying off the balances on the Discover, AmEx, and Visa cards, the balance on the MasterCard dropped from $6,000 to $4,013. Now our focus *and a lot more money* will go towards paying off this last card. When we add the $395 per month that we used to pay Visa to the initial $300 monthly MasterCard payment, we now pay $695 per month towards that balance. That's a huge jump!

Now watch what happens.

The remaining $4,013 will be paid off in only 7 months! Imagine – we barely made a dent in the MasterCard balance while we paid off the other cards, but now that our full attention is on this card, the total drops dramatically…and quickly.

WOW!!

Ultimately, by following this system, the four credit cards in our example are paid off *in four years and two months…or 50 months, if you prefer.* And this assumes no extra money gets kicked in toward any of these payments at any point in time.

"Oh, my God! Four years?!? I'll be *x* years old in four years!"

Well, how old will you be in four years if you *don't* pay off the credit cards?

Let's be positive and excited about this. In this example, $13,250 of principle and a significant amount of interest are paid off in less than four and a half years because of your disciplined approach. You avoided the credit cards and you followed the repayment plan.

You paid off this debt because *you wanted to pay off this debt.*

Everyone can do this. Just "Chip, Chip, Chip Away" at that debt!

Notes:

Notes:

CHAPTER SIX

GIVE...

When we are mired in debt, it is easy for us to feel sorry for ourselves and seek pity from everyone we talk to. It seems like every waking minute is wrapped up in fear and worry about this albatross. We have trouble sleeping at night, our conversations with family and friends eventually come around to debt, or at least money, in general, our production at work is limited by our obsession with credit cards, and even our leisure time in front of the TV is interrupted by thoughts of debt, especially when those commercials come on, tempting us to "buy now, pay later" – just whip out that credit card and "be happy." Yeah, right.

It's natural to be concerned about paying off what we owe. It is our responsibility to do so; we borrowed the money. At the same time, it is easy to do what I like to call "catastrophize over" our debt and the number of our credit cards that carry balances. Anger and frustration are common reactions to a "lifetime" of debt once we realize the negative effects that our abuse of credit has had on us.

But notice that concern, anger, and frustration, while reactions, all stem from negative thoughts: specifically, negative thoughts about ourselves. If unchecked, these thoughts lead to constant dejection and depression. This is unnecessary because we now have the tools to get ourselves out of debt in a logical and timely fashion.

To further insure that negative thoughts are kept in check, we need to "get our thoughts off ourselves" and onto other people and causes. Namely, we need to consider ways that we can help others and *give of ourselves*.

"Give? I'm in debt! Every dollar is accounted for."

Maybe. Maybe not. Now that you have created a written game plan and established a timetable for paying off your debts, you know how much discretionary income remains. Maybe there's none, but likely there's some, even if only a little.

Some people believe that they have to wait until they are completely or almost out of debt before they can/should start giving. I believe that we should start giving while we are in the "depths" of our debt. This limits the potential for creating a "woe-is-me" mentality, and it helps us to be grateful for the truly valuable "things" that we have, like our health, our family, etc. It also helps us to see that many people are even worse off than we are. Once a habit of genuine giving is started, it rarely ends. Genuine giving is a selfless act, coming from the heart, versus an obligatory act that we feel anxious about or burdened by. In fact, generosity tends to grow and over the years, we find ourselves giving more and more, which means either our income is increasing or we have reduced waste, which leaves us with more money than we used to have.

Remember that handy pad and pen you used to list your debts and interest rates? How can you forget? Well, get them again. This time, brainstorm a list of all the people and places where you might be able to give. Don't put much thought into this – just write. The art of brainstorming is to write spontaneously. Your list might include:

> your parents
> your siblings
> your church
> the local homeless shelter
> the local food pantry
> television ministries
> National Public Radio & TV
> overseas missions
> domestic causes
> The American Red Cross
> Feed the Children

To name just a few.

Of course, this list is not exhaustive. There are many more organizations and causes that can use your resources. You don't have to give to multiple causes or feel guilty about being able to give to just one or two. The choice is yours. Do what's in your heart.

If you have just a few dollars to give each month, that's fine. Don't be embarrassed by that. Embarrassment is a reflection of ourselves and our thoughts. Remember, the goal here is to focus our thoughts on others now. People and organizations with needs truly appreciate *anything* that we can give.

Now, let's say that you *truly* have no extra money to give. Again, this is no time for discouragement. We always have something to give. If you don't have money, you probably have time. Even one hour a week can make a huge difference in the life of a person in need. Maybe there is an elderly neighbor who cannot drive, or who has difficulty getting around. You can drive that person to the grocery store or to church. You can cut his/her lawn. You can cook dinner for that person once a week. There are numerous opportunities to help this person.

There are local organizations, from those that work with young children to those that cater to senior citizens, which need volunteers to help create enriching and happy experiences for their attendees. Giving of one's time is just as, and sometimes even more, rewarding as giving money.

Again, make a list – this time of the people you know (relatives, friends, neighbors, and so on) who can use your assistance. Be specific. Make another list of those local organizations, committees, schools, churches, etc., that can benefit from your assistance.

Once your lists are made, prioritize them. Which people do you feel could most use your help? Which ones do you feel most "compelled" to help? Do the same with your list of organizations, etc. Remember, volunteer work should not be drudgery. It should be rewarding! Then call these places to find out how you can be of service.

"Yeah, I've got an hour or two a week I can spare," you may say. "But I can't do anything for these people."

Yes, you can. You've probably spent so much time focusing on the mistakes you've made, such as creating a mountain of debt, that you've ignored your talents and abilities.

It's time for another list! Spend some time thinking about and writing down your talents and abilities. NOTHING is insignificant here. Don't belittle or deny the gifts and talents with which you were born and/or have developed over the years. Where to start? Well, what do you do for a living? Break down your job responsibilities and what you do on a daily basis. These skills may very well segue into a volunteer opportunity for you.

What are your hobbies? Why not share them with others? Maybe that hobby (or those hobbies) will fit the needs of some organization that would love to have you share your skills with its people.

Ironically, I'm asking you to put your mind back on yourself here, albeit temporarily. Because by thinking about what *you* can do and then *doing it*, you brighten the lives of others in need.

Even if you rationalize that you don't have *any* skills or talents, there is one thing that you definitely can do...you can listen! There are many people out there who are sad, discouraged, alone, and they simply want to talk. That's where you come in. If you can spend an afternoon or an evening a week with such a person, you will be making a difference in his or her life. Just knowing that you will be there to listen and to care will raise this person's self-esteem, even if just a little. In addition, you will feel great, knowing that you are having a positive impact on this person's life.

So *give of yourself*!

Notes:

Notes:

CHAPTER SEVEN

...AND "TAKE"?

You've heard of "the ol' give and take," right? Well, the "give" part was addressed in Chapter Six. Now, it's time for the "take." OK, let's soften that word a bit. By "take," I mean: *be open to RECEIVE.*

Many of us, especially when we are in debt, have a hard time receiving. We do not feel deserving of pay raises, gifts, or even compliments. We seem ungrateful or aloof, and this prevents us from experiencing "richer" lives. This attitude also stops people from giving more to us. And who can blame them? If we put ourselves in the giver's shoes, we would probably be upset if we did something nice for someone, and that person appeared unappreciative or ambivalent. Not that we should give simply to be thanked, but givers, like everyone else, have feelings and enjoy and deserve some recognition for their kindness. This recognition encourages them to continue giving.

Think of giving and receiving as a continuous channel. It is possible for one item to be given and received numerous times: one person giving to another who, in turn, gives to another, and so on. However, if somewhere along the line one person refuses to receive the item, the channel becomes blocked and further giving is prevented.

Also, think of it this way. If a giver's gift is rejected or unappreciated, the giver may be reluctant to give again, not just to this individual, but to anyone. Don't laugh – it happens. Again, we are human beings with feelings, and if our feelings are hurt, depending on how emotional or sensitive we are, this rejection could have a long-term, negative effect on us. We may say to ourselves, "I'm no fool! I remember what happened last time. I'm not going through that again!" We feel embarrassed when our generosity is ignored or not reciprocated.

The opposite can also happen. Many people who are in debt and live in lack create a poverty mentality for themselves. As a result, they fear letting go of possessions, afraid that they will have to do without. This, more than most things, clogs the giving and receiving channel. These people keep things that are broken, worn out, and no longer offer any pleasure, believing that they cannot afford to replace these objects.

You know, giving can be a lot like dating. Many of us have been in situations where we really wanted to go out with someone. But once we finally built up the courage to ask him/her out, we heard, "I want to be friends" (or something like that). Or maybe our offer for a date was accepted, but at the end of the evening or the next time we talked and asked for a second date, we were then rejected, either kindly or abruptly. Either way, it's painful.

A rejected gift is much like a rejected proposition. It can hurt the giver. Now don't get me wrong – I'm *not* saying that we should accept *every* date that we are asked on, nor should we take every item that is offered to us. That would lead to some boring evenings and a houseful of junk.

However, I am suggesting that we should consider the offer before we reject it outright. An outright rejection is often a "knee-jerk" reaction conditioned by our belief that we don't deserve the goodness and kindness offered to us. If after considering the offer you believe that there are "strings attached," or that the person making the offer is disingenuous, then by all means politely say, "No, thank you." You don't need to provide a reason unless you want to. Just go on with your life, knowing that you had the courage to say no. And you can feel good that you were noticed by another person!

Also, remember that to simply say "yes" because you have a hard time saying "no" adds nothing to your self-esteem, and you may very well kick yourself soon enough for not listening to your heart.

In the best case scenario, though, if the giver is genuine and is offering something of value that can improve your life, then think about it, and if you really want to accept the offer, do it! In all likelihood, both you and the other person will be happy, and you will start to feel better about yourself.

How good are you at receiving? And here I mean everything from gifts to compliments, even a simple "thanks." Maybe you haven't realized that you don't receive things easily. Let's do some introspection here. Shine the "light of awareness" on yourself and honestly answer the question that appears at the beginning of this paragraph. Write your responses. You may have several, considering that there are numerous ways in which things (objects, ideas) are offered. You don't need to share your responses to this exercise with anyone. This is just for you. But do it! You will learn something about yourself from the experience.

Review your responses. Are there any negative ones? How can you change those disempowering reactions to positive, affirmative responses?

Again, conditioned or "knee-jerk" reactions play a big role in our inability to receive easily. So, we need to put some thought into these situations. We need to feel comfortable when compliments, gifts, and recognition come our way. We need to "catch" them with a smile on our face. Chances are, the person who "threw" them to us was smiling, happy to offer his or her kindness.

We need to realize, first of all, that we are good people, deserving of *all* the abundance that life has to offer. This stops a lot of people right in their tracks because they do not see themselves in this way. Instead, they think, "Me? Abundant? What about my debt?" Remember, debt is a temporary situation that you are climbing out of, since you are now armed with the techniques and strategies already presented in this book. Also, debt is a reflection of your *past*...which is gone forever! Abundance and another important quality, prosperity, are the new benchmarks in your life.

You must believe that you are worthy of prosperity. You are, but do you *believe* that you are? Once that belief is genuine, then you will begin to *feel* it, which is much deeper and more permanent than simply *thinking* that we deserve it. Our strong feelings affect our actions. Like begets like. In the past, negative thoughts and feelings led to unproductive and self-sabotaging acts, like debting. Now, our positive attitudes about ourselves translate to productive actions, like saving, creating abundance, giving, receiving – add to the list yourself!

You now embody the qualities that make life full. By reconditioning yourself for abundance, you change the way you look at everything in your life and everything that may potentially enter your life. You'll start thinking differently about your relationships, your career, your dreams and aspirations, your religion/spirituality, your money, and your time, along with other aspects of your life.

A shift in consciousness makes all the difference here. When you see yourself as deserving of life's riches, you will realize that it is empowering to "take."

Notes:

Notes:

CHAPTER EIGHT

WHAT DO YOU WANT TO DO WITH YOUR LIFE?

Do you have a dream? What is it? Is it a dream job? A dream house?

Do you want to travel? Where do you want to go? Do you want to drive across America? Do you want to explore Europe? Do you want to go on a cruise? Fly half-way around the world?

Do you have a dream about money? I mean a *big* dream, not having "just enough" or paying your bills on time.

Well, when we are in debt, we tend to focus almost exclusively on how much we owe, and this results in a poverty mentality. When this happens, our dreams are squelched. We don't feel worthy of a better life, one that includes goals, desires, prosperity, abundance, and happiness. When we are in debt, all of our time and energy is spent keeping the creditors at bay and worrying about how we can stretch this paycheck until the next one comes around. There's a saying, "There's more month at the end of the money." Once we're debt free, though, we can turn that around to read, "There's more money at the end of the month." How does *that* feel? What would you do with that surplus?

But I think what's more important than the amount of money in your bank account is your day-to-day existence, your thoughts, your feelings, and who you are as a person. When you're out of debt, you can easily focus on a rich, fulfilling life without the fear of MasterCard, Visa, and all of their "evil cousins" mailing you their monthly greetings in the form of a bill. Honestly, I used to get a lot of mail. Now that I don't have credit card debt, my mail has gone down drastically. I like that!

With those albatrosses of debt and credit cards thrown off, see how much lighter you feel! Your head is no longer filled with so much negativity, nor is your body so stressed. You no longer have that tightness in your shoulders or that knot in your stomach. You get along better with your spouse or significant other, and the kids *actually like* spending time with you! All because you have mastered "the plastic hand grenades" that had previously caused so much destruction in your life.

You now have a sense of freedom. Money comes in...and look! You have the liberty to decide what to do with it! *You* get to keep, save, and give more of it. You can add to your savings account. You can build an emergency fund. Even though you are out of debt, emergencies still happen. You get to make "smart" purchases that can enhance your life. You can pay for school without taking out loans. You can buy new appliances without using those credit cards. You can throw out some of those old clothes and buy better outfits – and not worry about how you will pay for them. You now have the cash!

Then, of course, there are those questions I asked at the start of this chapter. People who are not in debt have a better chance of getting the job or career of their dreams than those who are in debt. Debtors often feel the need to stay in jobs they hate because "they pay the bills" or "the benefits are good." You've heard those excuses before, right? (Oh, *you've* used them?) Now, there are no more excuses!! Pursue your dreams!

If you are not happy at your job and you know that you are not doing what you were placed on this earth to do, you will not be completely content. Even if it is slight, there will be a nagging within, a feeling that you should be doing more, doing work that inspires you and others. Get out of that rationale about "paying the bills" and "good benefits." Nowadays, the benefits *stink* at many jobs! In many cases, these "benefits" don't even *exist* anymore! Maybe that's a good thing for those of us who want to leave our jobs and pursue our dreams. If the benefits stink, well, there's one excuse taken away. What about the bills? You plan to earn money at your dream career, too, right? Won't your dream career pay the bills?

"But I want to start my own business. That takes start-up money."

"I want to be an entrepreneur. I won't be able to rely on a steady paycheck at the beginning."

True and true. However, the amount of money needed upfront varies from start-up to start-up. Do some research on this before talking yourself out of business. And entrepreneurs can always apply for grants that can help "get the ball rolling." There are ways to live the life you want without standing on the proverbial bread line. A lot of these fears come as a result of the impoverished thinking from our debting days.

Also, now that you are climbing out of credit card debt, or maybe you are completely out of debt, you can take the money that used to go to the credit card companies and put it towards things like start-up expenses and an emergency fund while you create your dreams.

Remember, you're not quitting your job tomorrow (are you?). You can always start your dream business as a part-time venture. Seriously, having a passion is awesome, but just as you planned and charted a course to get out of credit card debt, you need to take "written action" when planning your dream and your future. This should *not* be drudgery. It should be exciting! This is *for you, not them* (the creditors)…or anyone else.

It's time for that pad again (those pad-makers are going to love me!). Start dreaming on paper. Brainstorm your dream career(s) – note the plural – yes, you can have more than one. I'm working on multiple dreams, as you'll soon see.

Set goals for yourself as to when you want to be out of your present situation and into your dream job, how much money you'll want, how much money you'll need, etc. Put this into a timeframe – be as specific as possible. If you aren't able to put a specific destination date next to your goals, then at least create a range that will stretch you a bit, but at the same time seem realistic to achieve.

Let's say you're reading this in January 2011. You might write, "I want to be out of _____
(write your present job here) within the next four months." Or, you might write, "by March 2011," or, "between January and March 2011." The more specific, the better. Also, putting goals and dreams on paper "brings them to life." Committing these things to writing also raises your level of accountability. You don't need to share this with anyone else, although an accountability partner, ideally someone whom you sincerely trust, can enhance your chances for successful completion of this endeavor. No matter what, you do need to be accountable *to yourself.* You are the one you have to sleep with every night. A guilty conscience or a feeling of inadequacy makes it very difficult to sleep – and you'll need a lot of energy to pursue your dream!

If you can dream it, you can achieve it. But you must plan it in order to share it. And "share" encompasses a lot of things. I'll let you think about that.

I've worked at jobs that I've hated, jobs that I've tolerated, and jobs that I've liked, but eventually got tired of. The jobs that fall into the first two categories coincided with the time when I was deeply in credit card debt. I made little money, and much of it went to our "friends" (you know who I'm talking about by now). I was the "middle man" with my own money: "taking" from my employer and "giving" to the credit card companies – this "take" and "give" *in no way* reflects the concepts addressed in chapters Seven and Six, respectively. You can see why.

I was frustrated because I worked simply to pay bills. As I stopped using the credit cards, my income did go up slightly, but more importantly, my debt went down, first slowly, then exponentially. As I saw "the light at the end of the tunnel" (freedom from debt), greater career choices opened up. I could focus more on doing what I liked and more on myself, in a positive, constructive way, because I no longer felt threatened by high finance charges and balances. I started teaching on the college level, which gave me the autonomy and independence I had never experienced while working in an office environment. I went from following the dictates of a hovering boss to influencing and inspiring college freshmen, many of whom were away from home for the first time in their lives. I now had the responsibility to help mold young men and women, a responsibility which I take *very seriously* to this day. And you had better believe that even though I am an English instructor, I've spent a significant amount of time talking with my students about the dangers of credit card debt.

I still enjoy teaching college students, but now it's time to "take it to the next level." Specifically, I want to go beyond the traditional classroom setting. As I write this book, I am starting a career as a professional and motivational speaker. My goal is to speak nationally and internationally on a number of topics, ranging from career transitioning to freedom from credit card debt.

In short, I want to make *the entire world* my classroom!

In addition to professional speaking and writing, I have begun to do voiceover work. You know – when you are watching TV or listening to the radio, and you hear the person who is either speaking "behind" the pictures or reading the copy? That's a voiceover artist. I am becoming one of those "voices." But voiceovers go beyond commercials. There are artists who narrate documentaries, do animated voices for cartoons, present "tags" – like James Earl Jones, who used to say, "This is CNN," in his deep, booming voice. There are even those who make recordings for telephone voicemail systems – "For Mr. Smith, press 1. For Ms. Jones, press 2…" And there are many other kinds of gigs as well.

I've also gotten into blogging. It's a great way to keep my writing skills sharp, as well as keep people informed. I invite you to one blog in particular:

http://saygoodbyetocreditcarddebtforever.blogspot.com.

Here, you will find ideas related to those that appear in this book. It also provides you an opportunity to interact with me by commenting on what you read on the blog.

But wait, there's more! Since I was a little kid, I have loved sports play-by-play announcing. I was the kid who would sit in front of the TV, hold a pencil like a microphone, and pretend he was calling the game. And I'll admit – I still do that sometimes. I'm not embarrassed to say that sports announcing is a dream of mine. It's a passion! I can't tell you how many times over the years that I've made a comment to my wife while we were watching a game, only to hear the announcer say the same thing, almost verbatim, just a few seconds later. That's *not* a fluke. That's a calling! I am pursuing this, too.

Of course, you don't have to have as many "irons in the fire" as I do. One iron can be enough if it's something you feel called to pursue, if it's something that excites you when you think about it. Only you can answer that for yourself. Only you *should* answer that for yourself.

There will be people who will tell you that you're foolish to follow your heart. Some will say it's too hard, it's impossible, it's never been done before, it's too late (for you), and it lacks security. Maybe you already heard this when you were younger and that is the reason why you put your dream "on hold." Know this – these negative people say these things because they don't see *themselves* doing them. They don't see themselves following their own dreams. So instead of taking responsibility for their own thoughts and inaction, they thrust their negativity onto you. Misery loves company, you know, so if they can pull you down to their level, they get some sort of perverse pleasure, because not only are they "losers," they want to make you one, too. DON'T LET THEM!! You know why it's "lonely at the top?" Because "the bottom," where they are, is OVERCROWDED!!

By the way, it's NOT lonely at the top. There are plenty of winners in the world. And there is plenty more room for another one. So Climb The Ladder To Success!

Will there be times when you may doubt yourself? Yes. Been There.

Will there be times when you feel that you're "too old?" Yes. Been There.

Will there be times when you just want to settle for something "easy?" Yes. Been There.

At the end of the day, is that what you really want? NO! You want to follow your dreams. I know – I'M THERE!

So…………………."WHAT DO YOU WANT TO DO WITH YOUR LIFE?"

Notes:

Notes:

CHAPTER NINE

NOW, THE END IS NEAR...

We have covered a lot of material in this book, from admitting to having a problem with credit cards, to realizing that a better life is now at hand. We have shifted our thoughts from negative and impoverished to positive and prosperous. Where we used to see problems, we now see opportunities. Overall, we have made dramatic changes in how we live because we have changed our habits with regard to credit cards.

And while the title of this chapter alludes to the fact that you have nearly reached the book's completion, this book is *not* meant to be read once and put on the shelf. It should serve as a resource and be referred to regularly, either as a reminder or reinforcement in some area, or as a motivational tool to get you back on track should you have a "bad" day or feel that your circumstances are "impossible." Everybody is entitled to a bad day once in a while. Occasionally, doubts will creep in. We are human beings, after all.

But just look at how much you have changed since you started reading this book (the first time)! You may have felt that you had no way out of credit card debt back then. Now look! You have a concise game plan mapped out that not only shows you how to take the necessary steps, but also explains that you can make your dreams come true and reach your goals in any area of your life – family, work, money, religion/spirituality – you name it!

So yes, "the end is near" as far as this book is concerned. But more importantly, you have reached the end of your poverty mentality. And with every ending comes a beginning. You are now starting a new and improved life, one that starts with productive thoughts, which lead to healthy actions and constructive habits. You are now inspired to see the best in *your* life and no longer envy what somebody else has. You are replacing fear with faith. You are experiencing joy where you used to feel pain.

What a wonderful, blessed life we live!

It's been a joy to share my knowledge and experience with you. I pray that you have been blessed by this book.

Now that you are living abundantly, I ask you to "pay it forward." If you know people who are struggling with credit card debt, please let them know that *there is a way out*. Share your newfound knowledge with them. Lead by example – let them know that life is hopeful, *not hopeless*. You may want to let a friend borrow your copy of this book or you might even want to buy a copy for a friend or relative…just be sure to pay cash!

You are blessed to be a blessing in their lives, just as I have been blessed in helping you.

Notes:

Notes:

CHAPTER TEN

"A FINAL WORD"

As I put the finishing touches on this book, an economic recession has greatly damaged the lives of many people around the world. Many millions of people have either lost their jobs or are working only part-time. Many are simply trying to make ends meet at any job whatsoever, putting their dreams on hold just to put food on the table. Thousands of houses have gone into foreclosure, and millions of dollars in savings have disappeared.

I won't go into more detail because details have already been, and continue to be, discussed in the media. Plus, this book has been about turning the negatives into positives, so focusing on the losses would be counterproductive and would counteract all the work we've done together. Suffice it to say, there are two ways to view this recession. Either we can wring our hands and take a "woe-is-me" attitude...or we can use it as a learning experience.

Is there anything we can do to prevent future national or worldwide recessions? On an individual basis, of course not. It seems to be "the nature of the beast" that after a period of increase comes a period of decrease, at least for the masses. But there are steps we can take in our own lives to alleviate some of the pressure when these difficult times occur. While I am not an economist or a finance expert, I can say with certainty and from experience that excessive use of credit cards will come back to haunt us at some time. This is definitely true when the world experiences hard economic times. Maybe we are "forced" to use credit cards for a brief period due to a loss of income or a medical emergency – that's understandable. But what about the "good" times? What about when we're working full-time, or when we have two or more incomes in the household? How are we using our credit cards then? Are we using them recklessly and unconsciously? Are we carrying balances? Are we wasteful? Seeking instant gratification? If the answer is "yes" to any or all of these questions, then there will definitely be a problem when the bottom drops out. We're seeing that now. Thoughtless habits get us into trouble…maybe not today or tomorrow, but eventually.

As individuals, we need to take responsibility for how we spend. When it comes to money, each of us has to pay attention to how we use it, whether it's the money we actually have or the money we borrow. We must also watch how we use our credit cards.

Thousands of people have gotten into trouble through their abuse of credit cards. We have been irresponsible. To make matters worse, banks and credit card companies made it "too easy" for us to open credit card accounts, to increase our limits, and to make only minimum payments. The banks issuing these credit cards have made millions of dollars "on the backs of 'ignorant' consumers" – in short, they took advantage. They abused us…and *we* let it happen! In effect, they were irresponsible, too.

Fortunately, the Congress of the United States, under the insistence of President Barack Obama, created the CARD Act of 2009 (CARD stands for "Credit Card Accountability and Responsibility and Disclosure"). President Obama signed it into law in May 2009. The law took full effect in August 2010.

By law, banks and credit card companies are now held accountable for how they treat their customers. Agreements must be written "in plain language" (not legalese), and issuers must provide, as stated in a White House press release from May 2009, "Real information about the Financial Consequences of Decisions: Issuers will be required to show the consequences to consumers of their credit decisions" (www.whitehouse.gov).

The complete CARD Act can be read online, but the following points highlight some of the key features and changes that have taken effect:

*Cardholders are protected against arbitrary interest rate increases. Card companies must give cardholders 45 days notice of any interest rate increases.

*Retroactive interest rate increases are banned, except when a cardholder is more than 60 days late paying a credit card bill.

*Universal Default is eliminated. In the recent past, if you were late on one bill, credit card companies could raise your interest rates, even if the late payment was NOT related to their card. No longer!!

*Credit card companies can no longer arbitrarily change the terms of the contract with the cardholder.

*Cardholders who pay on time should not be penalized. Companies cannot charge interest on payments made during the grace period. No more "double-cycle" billing.

*Companies must mail billing statements 21 calendar days before the due date; previously the law was 14 days.

*The due date must be the same date each month.

*Companies cannot charge late fees when a cardholder proves that payment was mailed within seven days of the due date.

*Cardholders have the right to set limits to their credit. This prevents companies/banks from charging over-the-limit fees on a cardholder who has a fixed credit limit.

*Card companies should *fairly* credit and allocate payments. Payments are made to the debt with the *highest* interest rate *first*. Previously, most companies required consumers to pay off the *lowest* interest-rate balance first.

*Vulnerable consumers are protected from Fee-Heavy *SUBPRIME* credit cards. ALL fees for subprime cards, whose total fixed fees over a year *exceed 25 percent* of the credit limit, must be paid up front *before the card is issued.*

NOTE – As a college instructor for many years, I am especially grateful for the next few changes:

*No credit card may be issued to a consumer under the age of 21 unless the applicant has an adult co-signer (like a parent or a guardian), or can prove a means of paying off the debt.

*College students must receive parental (or a guardian's) permission in order to get an increase in their credit lines on joint accounts held with those adults.

*People under 21 years old will be protected from pre-screened offers, unless they specifically opt-in for offers.

*Card companies cannot induce students to sign up (i.e. – NO MORE FREE T-SHIRTS!).

*Institutions of higher education must publicly disclose any agreement made with the card issuer to market a card on campus.

BUT WAIT – THERE'S MORE!

Yes, there's MUCH more to the CARD Act. Since I have been emphasizing responsibility and pro-activity throughout this book, it would be a great idea to go to the Web and read the CARD Act. If you google it or go to Wikipedia, you can find and read it.

Suffice it to say, I am thrilled that the banks and credit card companies are FINALLY being held accountable for their selfish and immoral behavior. But when all is said and done, we, the consumers, need to take control of and responsibility for our financial behavior.

Let's learn from our "mis-steps." Let's change for the better. Let's come out of this recession as prosperous people who have grown from challenging experiences.

I WISH YOU ALL AN ABUNDANT, DEBT FREE LIFE.

Notes:

Notes:

Notes:

_____

_____

_____

_____

_____

_____

_____

_____

_____

_____

_____

_____

_____

_____

_____

_____

_____

_____

_____

_____

_____

_____

_____

_____

_____

_____

Notes:

Notes:

Notes:

Notes:

ABOUT THE AUTHOR

Joe Paretta is an author, speaker, and teacher. He has taught at the college level since 1996 and also tutored for 20 years. This is the first of several books that he plans to write on various topics. Joe and his wife, Jessica, live in Jim Thorpe, Pennsylvania. They purchased a home in their dream location of the Pocono Mountains after divesting themselves of their own credit card debt.

Catch up with Joe on Twitter, Facebook, LinkedIn, and on his blog, http://saygoodbyetocreditcarddebtforever.blogspot.com. Stay connected for information on Joe's forthcoming Web site: www.joeparetta.com. See you there!